KW-176-694

GIANTS OF THE AIR

David Jefferis

Illustrated by
Terry Hadler
Ron Jobson and Michael Roffe

Franklin Watts
London   New York   Toronto   Sydney

First published in 1988 by
Franklin Watts
12a Golden Square
London W1R 4BA

First published in the USA
by Franklin Watts Inc.
387 Park Avenue South
New York, N.Y. 10016

First published in Australia
by Franklin Watts
Australia
14 Mars Road
Lane Cove, NSW 2066

UK ISBN: 0 86313 669 9
US ISBN: 0-531-10564-4
Library of Congress
Catalog Card No: 87-51695

Technical consultant
Tim Callaway, RAF Museum,
Hendon, London

Designed and produced by
Sunrise Books

© 1988 Franklin Watts

Printed in Belgium

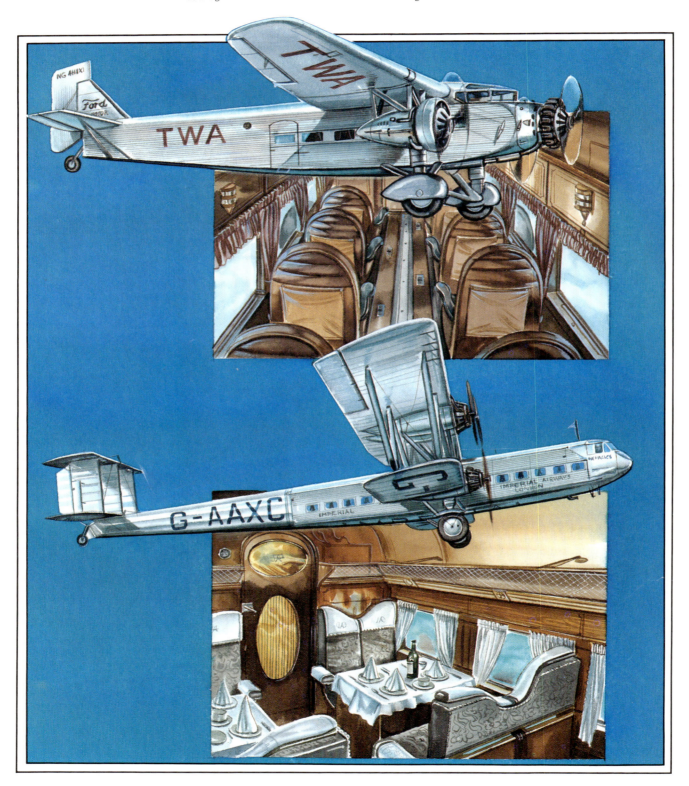

HACKNEY COLLEGE LIBRARY

H068369

ACC. No	HO68369
CLASS No	629.133 JEF
LOCATION	D
TYPE	BICL

GIANTS OF THE AIR

Contents

Introduction

The story of commercial flying has been dominated by speed, cost and safety. The first airliners were little faster than railway trains, and often slower in bad weather. Few aircraft could make cross-ocean flights until after World War II. Then came the jet age and the boom in air travel. Today, cost is more important than speed as most people wish to fly cheaply. Constant improvements in engine reliability, airframe design and precision navigation have resulted in a good safety record for the world's airlines. Unfortunately accidents do happen but all airlines have flight safety as a top priority. A typical jet liner is reliable enough to be in service for 20 years or more.

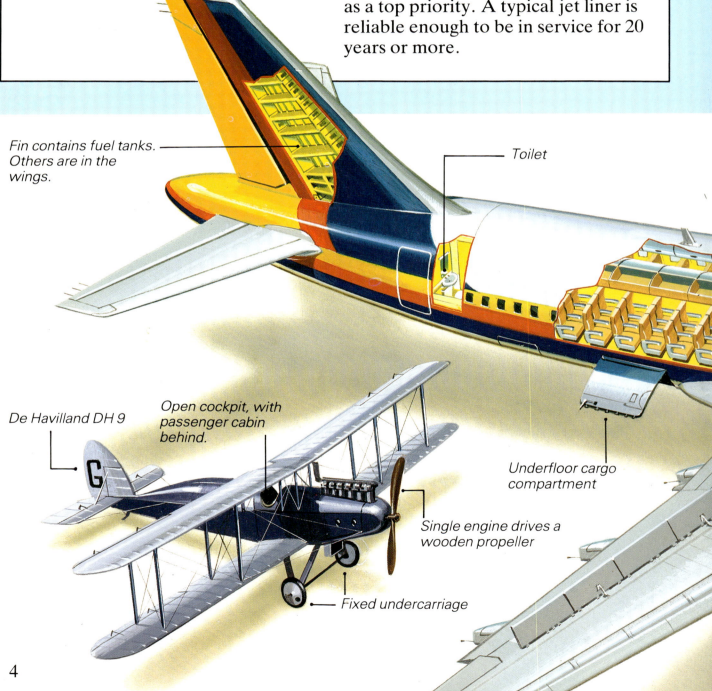

Fin contains fuel tanks. Others are in the wings.

Toilet

De Havilland DH 9

Open cockpit, with passenger cabin behind.

Underfloor cargo compartment

Single engine drives a wooden propeller

Fixed undercarriage

4

Airliners old and new

These two airliners represent two extremes of technical development. The small biplane is a De Havilland DH 9, converted from a World War I medium bomber. The pilot sat in an open cockpit while his passengers sat in an unheated cabin.

The jetliner is an Airbus A320, built by a group of European aircraft manufacturers. It contains the latest in technical advances. The meters and dials of the cockpit instrument panel are replaced by computer-controlled TV screens. Flight control is computer-assisted too. If the computers sense that a pilot is flying the jet into a dangerous flight position, they will override the pilot's commands to keep the plane on a safe course.

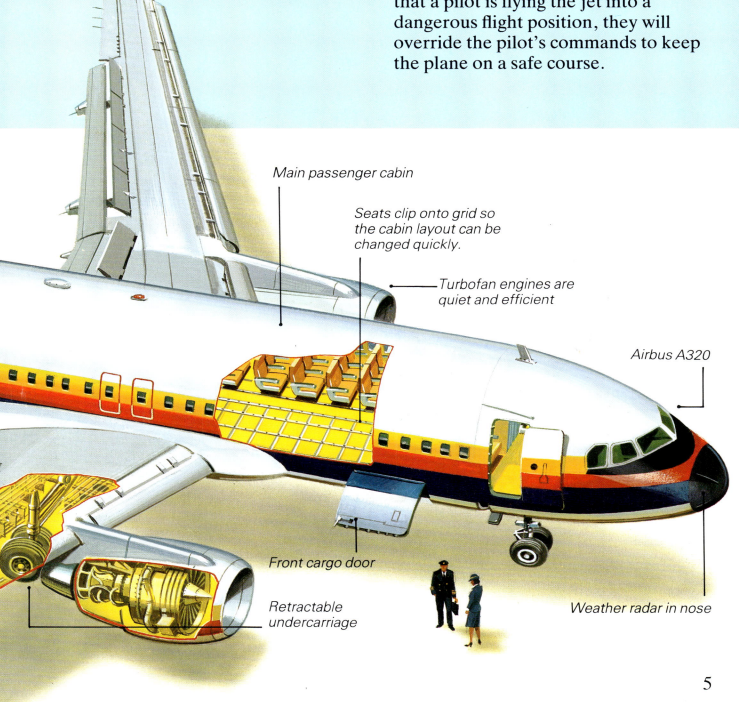

Main passenger cabin

Seats clip onto grid so the cabin layout can be changed quickly.

Turbofan engines are quiet and efficient

Airbus A320

Front cargo door

Retractable undercarriage

Weather radar in nose

5

The first passenger flights

In 1903, the Wright brothers became the world's first aviators when they piloted their *Flyer* into the air. The next few years saw tremendous advances in aviation, but the first daily aircraft passenger service did not start until 1914.

The Benoist Aircraft Company was based at St Louis in the United States. The plan was to provide a local service between the two towns of St Petersburg and Tampa in Florida. On New Year's Day, 1914, pilot Anthony Jannus took off with Mayor Pheil of St Petersburg as passenger. The Benoist Type XIV flying boat cruised at 103 km/h (64 mph) and the 35-km (22-mile) flight took only 23 minutes.

The St Petersburg and Tampa Airboat Line made two or more return trips a day. Passengers were charged $5 a flight, though people weighing more than 91 kg (200 lb) were charged extra.

A total of 1,205 passengers were carried with only 22 flight cancellations. This was a good record, as aircraft of the time had unreliable engines and were easily grounded by bad weather.

In late April 1914, the Airboat Line was shut down as it was not a big money-spinner. Two years later Tony Jannus was killed in a flying accident while serving in Europe during World War I. By the end of the war, the Benoist company had gone out of business, but many other people were ready to start their own airlines.

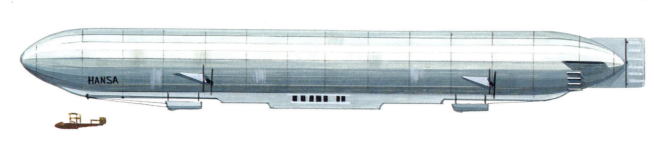

Benoist XIV to scale

The 1914 Air Boat Line was the first to use aeroplanes, but airship services were started five years before. In Germany Graf Ferdinand von Zeppelin had been experimenting with airship designs since 1900 and on October 16, 1909, the airship transport company DELAG was formed. Several of the huge craft were destroyed in crashes caused by engine failures, storms and fires. Even so, the airship *Hansa* pioneered the first international airship flight, between Germany and Sweden. DELAG's flights went on until the start of World War I in August 1914.

▽ *The Benoist Type XIV was a small two-seat flying boat. Its engine was low-mounted to give good stability in the air and on the water. It had an open cockpit, so pilot and passenger wore warm clothes and goggles.*

Early airliners

Civil aviation really got going after World War I. The first airliners were converted bomber designs. The Vimy bomber that made the first transatlantic flight in 1919 had its airliner version too. The Vimy Commerical had a chubby fuselage containing seats for ten passengers. It also had a toilet, the first airliner to have one.

In the 1920s, bad weather caused many delays and dangers. In haze or mist pilots often followed railway lines or roads to avoid getting lost. On April 7, 1922, a De Havilland 18 airliner was flying from London to Paris, its crew peering through the cloud to the ground below, trying to keep on course. Unknown to the British crew, a French Farman Goliath was flying

towards them, heading for London. The French crew were also looking down at the ground.

Over the village of Thieuloy-Sainte-Antoine in northern France, the two aircraft flew straight into each other. Destruction was total and wreckage was strewn over a wide area. There were no survivors of this first midair collision between airliners.

After this tragic accident, the idea of air corridors was put into action. Aircraft had to stay in separate airlanes to avoid collisions, and captains had to file a flight plan before each takeoff, so that ground controllers would know when and where they were going.

A flat grass field for takeoff and landing, plus some hangars and a customs shed, was all most airports ran

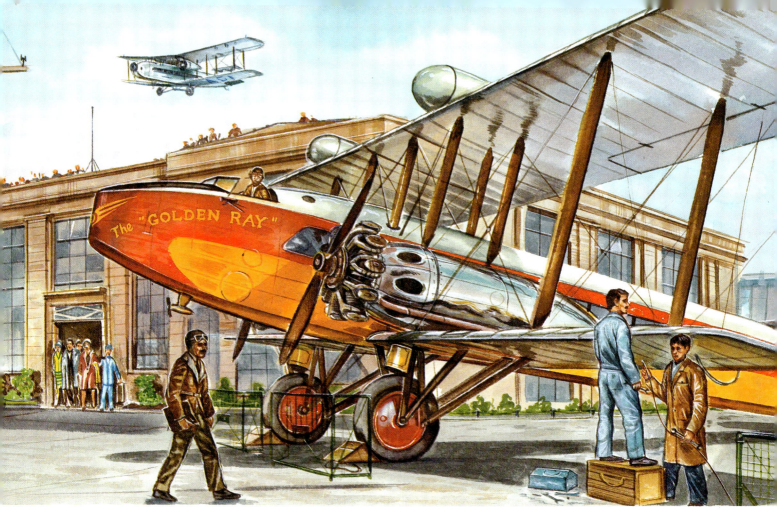

△ Flying past the control tower at Croydon is a Junkers F13. The German aircraft was first all-metal airliner. The Golden Ray was a London to Paris service operated by the French airline Air Union. The plane taking off is a Vimy Commercial, based on a famous World War I bomber design.

to in the 1920s. One of the best was at Croydon, south of London. Here, London's main airport boasted a splendid terminal building and control tower. There were no runways as grass was all the aircraft needed. Planes were not heavy enough to require concrete. Maintenance was quite simple – Croydon's grass was cut twice a year by horse-drawn mower until 1926, when a motor tractor was bought for the job.

Today, maintaining the long runways needed by huge jetliners is a complex and expensive job.

△ The Golden Ray was a flying restaurant, used on London to Paris flights. It was the most luxurious plane of the day. Three stewards looked after a dozen passengers, serving them with a six-course lunch. There was also a selection of fine wines on board.

Air progress

At the start of the 1920s, comfort for crews and passengers hardly existed. Most airliners had open cockpits and except on special luxury services, passengers crammed into draughty, unheated cabins.

Enclosed cockpits improved crew comfort – though many pilots liked to feel the wind against their skin, reasoning that they could control the plane better that way – while wicker chairs and in-flight food helped the

▷ The Ford Tri-motor carried 11–14 passengers in wicker seats. Over 200 were built. The Handley Page HP 42, with its biplane design, looked old-fashioned even on its first flight in 1930. But the HP 42 was built with passenger comfort in mind and give people a safe and comfortable flight.

passengers during their noisy and often bumpy flights.

Early commercial aircraft were expensive to buy and operate. In Europe government subsidies backed most airline operations. In the United States airmail contracts were awarded to airlines, enabling them to make a profit. At first, passengers were regarded as a nuisance, compared to uncomplaining bags of mail!

During the 1920s, planes designed purely as airliners took to the air, including the Ford Tri-motor which first flew in 1926. Nicknamed the "Tin Goose" for its corrugated metal construction, the Ford was tough and reliable, though very noisy to fly in. Before long, the popular Ford was used by all the major American airlines. Trans World Airlines used the plane for the first United States coast-to-coast service, a trip that took 36 hours.

▽ The first airline captains sat in open cockpits, so they dressed like World War I fighter pilots, with goggles and flying jackets. Naval-style uniforms were introduced in the early 1920s and have changed little since. Air stewardesses first flew in 1930, their job to care for the passengers.

In 1930, Boeing Air Transport, later part of United Airlines, introduced the world's first air stewardesses. They were trained as nurses, to care for the many passengers who became airsick when the small planes flew into rough weather. The girls helped in other ways too. They often helped to refuel planes, carry baggage and clean cabin floors.

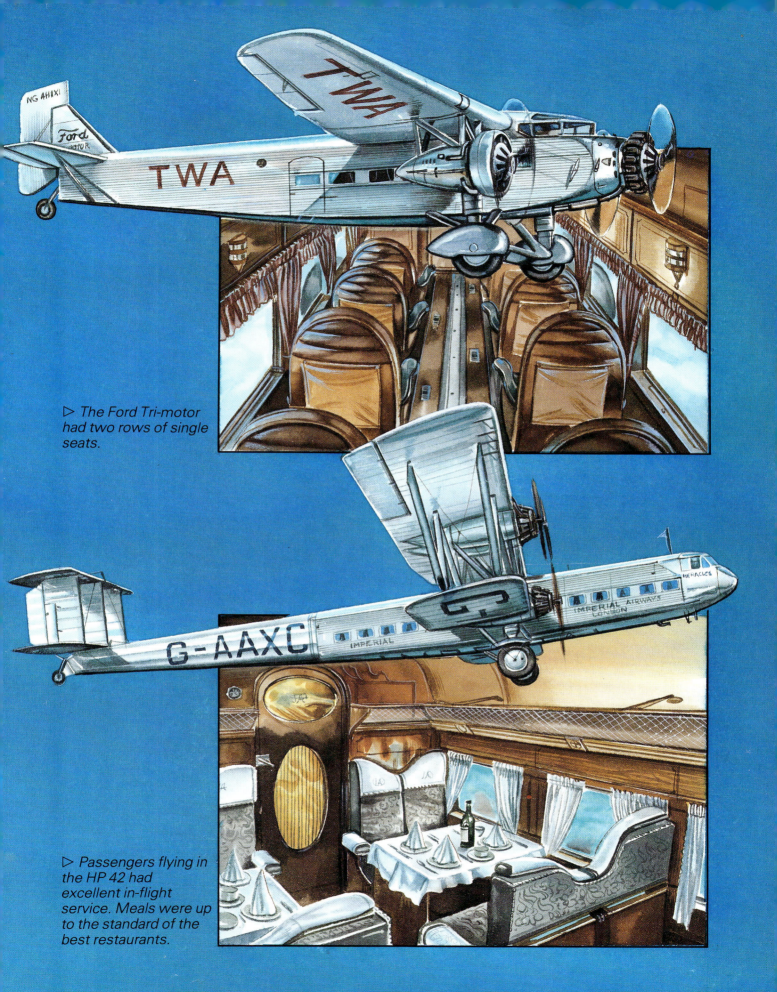

▷ The Ford Tri-motor had two rows of single seats.

▷ Passengers flying in the HP 42 had excellent in-flight service. Meals were up to the standard of the best restaurants.

The Douglas DC-3

One December afternoon in 1935, a gleaming new twin-engined aircraft rolled out of its hangar, ready for its maiden flight.

The plane was the Douglas DC-3, designed as a fast passenger transport for American Airlines, which had ordered 20. The aircraft first went into service in June 1936, flying non-stop from New York to Chicago.

The designers didn't imagine that the DC-3 would become the most successful transport plane ever, with over 13,000 being built. In fact the plane was designed with just a 50-aircraft production run in mind. In World War II, thousands were built as the C-47 military transport. The last DC-3 was built in 1948, but over 1,000 are still in flying condition.

The DC-3 is a 28–32 seater but more passengers have been carried on a least one emergency flight. In 1942, a DC-3 was taking Major Jimmy Doolittle from China to India. The pilot landed in Burma to pick up some refugees and the cabin was packed with dozens of homeless people. The plane staggered into the air and lumbered on to India. After a heavy landing, Doolittle, five crew and 59 refugees jumped out. Then another dozen people appeared – they had all squeezed into the rear baggage compartment!

On another occasion, a bomb-damaged DC-3 had a wing replaced with one from a smaller DC-2. The new wing was nearly two metres (6 ft) shorter than the proper one, but the "DC-2½" made a successful flight.

Age of the airship

The airship was queen of the skies in the years between the wars. In October 1929, the huge Graf Zeppelin crossed the Atlantic for the first time. In mid-ocean, storm winds ripped some fabric off the fin, making control very difficult. Crew members climbed out to replace the material, clinging desperately to the airship's metal girders as they worked 250 m (820 ft) above the heaving Atlantic waves. The Graf made the trip in 11 hours 43 minutes, carrying 62,000 pieces of mail and 20 passengers. The Graf Zeppelin went to complete many safe journeys, a fate which was not shared by its sister ship, the Hindenburg. On May 6, 1937, the Hindenburg exploded as it came in to land at Lakehurst, New Jersey: 35 passengers and crew died in the blaze. The tragic crash ended the age of the airship.

Today's airships use helium, a gas which does not catch fire.

◁ The 1933 Boeing 247 (left) could carry 10 passengers. It was far superior to the biplanes of the time but the Douglas "DC" planes were even better. The DC-1 could carry four more passengers for the same operating cost, while the 32-seat DC-3 (above) went on to become the most successful airliner ever.

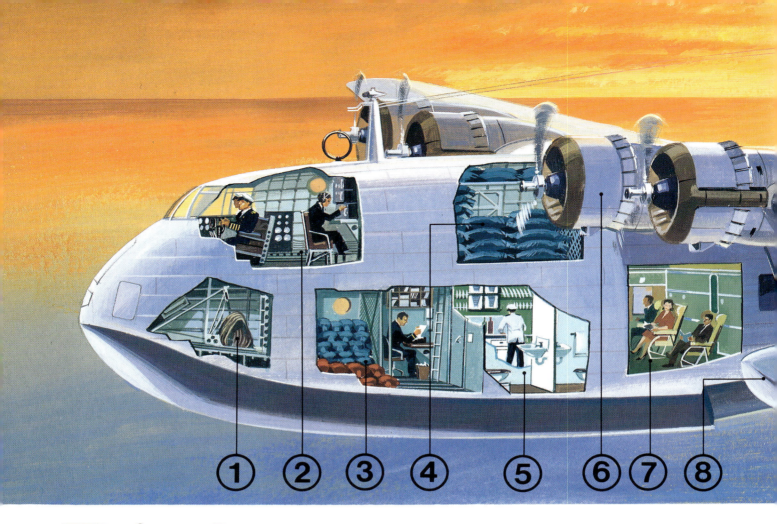

① ② ③ ④ ⑤ ⑥ ⑦ ⑧

Flying boats

Among the pioneers of flying boat services were the Frenchman Pierre Latécoère and Charles Lindbergh, the American who flew the Atlantic solo in 1927.

After the flight, Pan American Airways signed up Lindbergh to fly test routes to Central and South America. The flights were highly successful and by 1930, Pan Am had routes through 15 countries. Latécoère started an airmail link between Africa and Brazil.

The 1930s were the golden age of flying boats. They could moor at harbours around the world, using the sea as a runway. The unlimited takeoff length of the open water meant that flying boats could be made bigger than land-based planes. This gave room to carry fuel for long-distance flights and lots of space for passengers.

The boats were competitors to the huge ocean liners of the time, and they rivalled ships in comfort and elegance, something few landplanes could equal.

The most comfortable flying boat of all was the Short C-class Empire boat. From the Imperial Airways seaplane base at Southampton, the boats flew to destinations across the world.

You were well looked after in an Empire boat. You sat in a soft seat, the

engines making no more than a hum as the passenger cabins had double soundproofing. The floor was thickly carpeted and the rest of the cabin was decorated to match. If you wanted to stretch your legs, you could go to the promenade deck and look out of the big windows. There was usually a splendid view as the boats rarely flew higher than 1,525 m (5,000 ft). Meals were freshly cooked by the flight steward in the tiny galley.

Night flights were made, but most flying was during the daytime and boats were normally moored for the night. Passengers were put up in luxury hotels for a good night's sleep and the flight would resume after breakfast the following morning.

Inside an Empire boat

The Empire boats of Imperial Airways gave passengers standards of comfort which have never been bettered. Passengers sat in large armchairs, there was a promenade deck and fresh food was specially prepared for each meal.

1 Compartment holds mooring equipment.
2 Flight deck for the captain, first officer and radio operator. There was also a ship's purser and a steward.
3 Mail compartment. The boat carried over a tonne of mail, plus baggage.
4 Upper mail compartment.
5 Galley.
6 Four Bristol Pegasus engines.
7 Midship cabin.
8 Metal hull and wingtip float.
9 Promenade cabin.
10 Aft cabin. The boat could carry up to 24 passengers.
11 Mail, freight and baggage hold.

The stowaway

When World War II broke out in September 1939, airlines mostly went onto a war footing, people and planes being taken over for military purposes. Transatlantic flights were for VIPs or military officers but Elizabeth Drewry was neither.

She was a flight mechanic at Prestwick airfield in Scotland and wanted to be a pilot but had no qualifications. She decided to apply in the United States where the rules were not quite so strict. You couldn't buy an air ticket in wartime Britain, so Elizabeth decided to stow away on a westbound plane.

On the cold, wet night of November 19, 1942, Captain Geordie Stewart revved up the four engines of his Liberator bomber, converted for passenger carrying. In the dark, Elizabeth Drewry sprinted past the Liberator's tailplane, under the fuselage and heaved herself up into the nosewheel bay. There was not much room – tanks full of de-icing fluid to one side, nose wheel in front, and immediately behind her was the back of the pilot's instrument panel. Looking through a gap in the panel, she could

▽ *Captain Stewart didn't see Elizabeth Drewry running past his cockpit towards the nosewheel bay. Once there, it was easy for her to climb up inside the hiding place.*

see the pilot's and flight engineer's feet!

Then Captain Stewart opened up the engines and the plane roared along the runway. After takeoff the nose wheel, still spinning, retracted up next to Elizabeth. The bay doors shut and she breathed a sigh of relief – she was on her way. But she couldn't relax, as there was standing room only. She dared not sleep on the de-icer tanks in case the doors opened and she fell out.

In fact, she was lucky to survive at all. Liberators usually flew at 7,000 m (20,000 ft) with passengers and crew all wearing oxygen masks. On this night, favourable winds were much lower, below 1,524 m (5,000 ft). Had Stewart flown at normal altitude, Elizabeth would almost certainly have died for lack of oxygen.

After 13 hours of cold, discomfort, hunger and boredom, Elizabeth felt the Liberator nose down for landing at Gander in Newfoundland. After refuelling, the plane took off again, heading for its final destination, Montreal in Canada.

After touchdown at Montreal, the plane was towed into a hangar and Elizabeth got out, stiff and tired. Then, as she made for the hangar exit, a voice called out "Where did you crawl from?" She was caught . . .

Later, Canada's Immigration Board allowed her to stay in the country for six months. She went to the United States and learnt to fly but still no air service wanted her as a pilot. She had failed in her main aim, but had flown "the pond" successfully and had earned her pilot's wings!

High-altitude flight

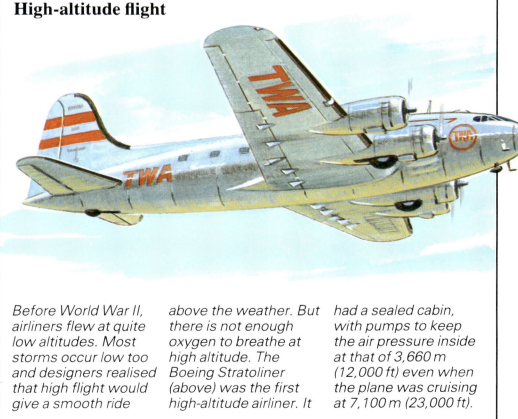

Before World War II, airliners flew at quite low altitudes. Most storms occur low too and designers realised that high flight would give a smooth ride above the weather. But there is not enough oxygen to breathe at high altitude. The Boeing Stratoliner (above) was the first high-altitude airliner. It had a sealed cabin, with pumps to keep the air pressure inside at that of 3,660 m (12,000 ft) even when the plane was cruising at 7,100 m (23,000 ft).

Jetliners

Jet-powered aircraft were first flown during World War II. Work on jets continued after the war and in 1949 the first jet airliner was ready.

On July 27, the De Havilland Comet took to the air, and the sleek machine broke many records. On October 25, 1949, a Comet flew from England to Libya. Coming back, it flew at 735 km/h (457 mph), much faster than any prop plane.

Several airlines ordered Comets and BOAC started the world's first jet passenger service on May 2, 1952. For almost two years all went well, then disaster struck.

In January 1954, a Comet crashed into the sea after takeoff from Rome. In April, another Comet went down in the sea near Naples. All Comets were grounded and Royal Navy ships recovered most of the first wreck.

The pieces were reassembled at Farnborough, England, while another Comet was put into a test tank. In this, water was pumped into the fuselage to create strains similar to those of high altitude flight. The fuselage split apart and the cause of the crashes was discovered. Cracks had spread from a rivet hole by a window, causing the cabin to explode.

The cracks were caused by metal fatigue, something that aircraft designers hadn't thought about until these crashes. Aircraft are now designed to keep it under control and inspections for cracks are a vital part of aircraft maintenance.

△ The De Havilland Comet had four jet engines buried in the wings.

△ Flight recorders are now carried on all big jets. In flight, a recorder keeps track of speed, height, and other information. It is water and fireproof and if recovered after a crash, its data can give vital clues to the cause.

◁ The prototype Boeing 707 flew on July 15, 1954. The four-engined jet became a best-seller, cruising at around 886 km/h (550 mph).

△ The Sud Aviation Caravelle was the first jet to have its engines mounted at the tail.

△ The Lockheed Constellation cruised at 496 km/h (308 mph).

▽ The Douglas DC-7C was the first airliner able to fly London to New York non-stop.

△ The Vickers Viscount was the first turboprop airliner.

▽ The Fokker Friendship is a turboprop airliner for short haul routes.

Long-distance propeller airliners were used by the airlines in the 1950s. They were eventually replaced by the faster jets, but aircraft such as the 1943 Constellation and 1955 DC-7C gave reliable service for many years. The 1953 Viscount had turboprop engines. The quiet and economical turboprop uses a jet engine to turn a propeller. It is a popular powerplant for short-range airliners, including the Fokker Friendship.

Airports

A modern international airport is a complex place. O'Hare airport at Chicago in the United States is the world's busiest, handling nearly 48 million passengers and 750,000 takeoffs and landings every year.

Freight is important too and most airliners carry freight containers under the passenger cabins. London's Heathrow airport handles about 500,000 tonnes of freight a year.

At the heart of every airport is the control tower. From here, all aircraft movements in the air and on the ground are watched on radar. Ground and air traffic controllers direct the aircraft by radio.

Airports also have huge fuel stores, maintenance hangars, cargo handling areas, fire fighting equipment and medical services. Passenger terminals include check-in and customs areas. Because of the threat of hijack by terrorists, officials check passengers with X-ray videos and machines which can detect guns and explosives.

▷ *Air travel is very safe, but takeoff and landing are moments of hazard during any flight. If an engine fails or a sudden sidewind or downdraught blows an aircraft off-course, there is little time to take emergency action. Bad weather landings can be hazardous but the ILS instrument landing system is an important safety aid.*

Radio signals from transmitters based at the airport move two needles on an instrument in the cockpit. When the needles form a cross, the plane is lined up correctly. Red and white lights positioned at the beginning of the runway signal if the airliner is approaching too high or too low.

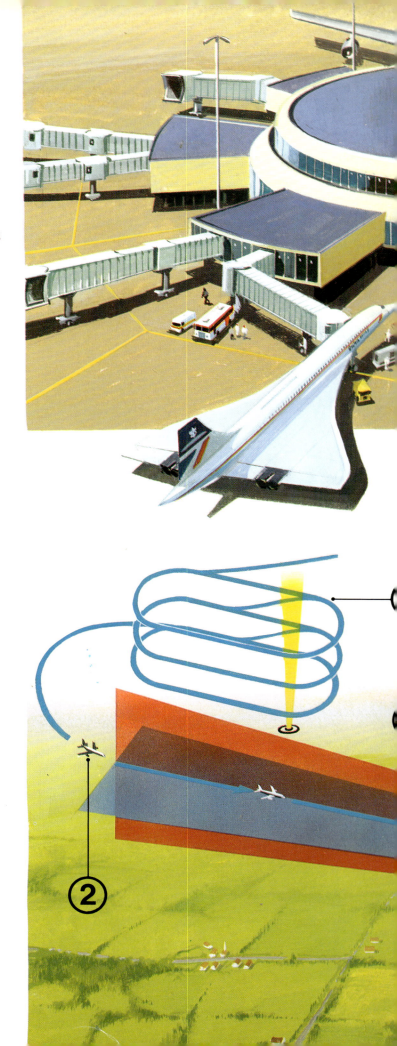

Jetway

△ Here you see jetliners parked at the passenger terminal of a modern airport.

After landing, an aircraft pilot noses his plane near the terminal before turning off the engines. Then jetways swing round to link the terminal directly to the front passenger door of the aircraft.

Using a jetway, passengers do not have to walk down stairs or across tarmac. They simply walk through the jetway tunnel straight into the terminal building.

Once inside, passport and baggage checks are made before passengers can leave the airport.

1 Aircraft waiting to land are "stacked" until the runway is clear.
2 An aircraft ordered off the stack turns towards the runway.
3 Radio beams of ILS system line up the aircraft on the glideslope. When on course, the plane flies in a shallow sloping line to the runway.
4 Radio markers indicate distance from runway.
5 Runway.
6 Airport.

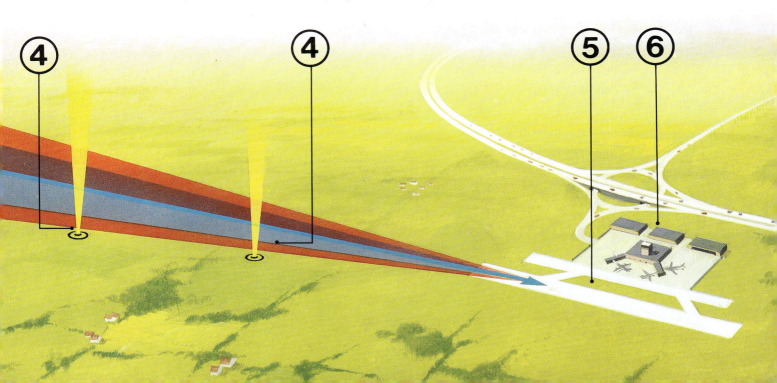

Wide-body jets

The success of the first jetliners led to a big boom in air travel. From being a rich man's luxury, air flight became the normal way to travel long distances. But fuel prices rocketed in the early 1970s so jets had to be designed that used less fuel.

The answer from Boeing was the huge model 747, with a wide body carrying over 500 people and powered by newly developed, quiet and economical turbofan engines. Although wide-body airlines are expensive to buy – the 1987 cost of a 747 is about $100 million – they give a

flying cost per seat about that of a private car. So seat prices can be kept low and more people can buy tickets.

Other manufacturers brought out wide-body jets too. Lockhead made the TriStar and McDonnell Douglas the DC-10. Both of these had three engines. Later, France led a group of European manufacturers called Airbus Industrie to produce another wide-body design, the A300. Airbus now makes a whole range of aircraft types and competes head-on with the American manufacturers.

Making aircraft such as these is a

The best selling jet

The twin-engined 737 is the baby of the Boeing jetliner family. In 1987, it outsold Boeing's other bestseller, the 727, to become the most widely ordered jet airliner ever. By September 1987 orders for the 737 stood at 1,903.

The most stretched jet

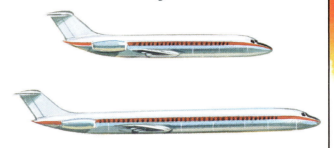

The McDonnell Douglas DC-9 started off as an 80–90 seater, measuring 31.82 m (104 ft) in length. Bigger engines and fuselage plugs have resulted in a 179-seater measuring 45.06 m (148 ft). The DC-9 is now known as the MD-80.

△ This is the latest development of the three-engine DC-10, renamed the MD-11. The small picture shows the passenger cabin of a typical wide-body. They all follow a similar layout with two aisles and big overhead lockers for passengers' coats and bags.

The quietest jet

The British Aerospace 146 has four Avco Lycoming engines slung under its high-mounted wings. The engines are so quiet that the plane can make night flights to airports that normally ban jets after dark because of the noise they make.

highly complex business, with no single firm making a complete machine. The Boeing 747 is made of about 4½ million parts. These are made and supplied by 1,500 separate companies, based in countries as far apart as the United States, Japan and Ireland. Companies making parts often share some of the commercial risk, reaping their profit if the plane is a winner.

Wide-body airliners are no faster than earlier planes (some are slower) but because they move large numbers of people cheaply, the airlines will carry on using them.

The flight of BA 009

It was a dark night on June 24, 1982, as British Airways flight BA 009 flew over Java, heading towards Perth in Australia. There was no unusual weather forecast, yet the flight crew watched a weird lighting display. Millions of glowing sparks were hitting the windshield of their Boeing 747. Looking out of the side windows, Captain Eric Moody saw the engines and wings surrounded with a bright glow. Then the right outer engine backfired, surged and died.

In the passenger cabins, the view outside was terrifying – the wings seemed encased in dancing flames, while explosions and sheets of white fire spurted out of the engines. Inside, acrid black smoke poured into the cabin. A minute after the first engine failure, a second engine died, followed rapidly by the remaining two.

In the sudden quiet, Moody pushed the 747's nose down to maintain speed and the great plane, weighing over 300 tonnes, glided down through the night air. From the cruising height of 11,278 m (37,000 ft) to sea level would take over 20 minutes, so there was time to try and restart the engines.

The mighty Boeing 747

When the Boeing 747 first flew on February 9, 1969, it was the biggest jetliner ever. It remains so today, and the latest 747-400 version seats over 400 passengers. The main deck is 57 m (187 ft) long, a distance greater than the Wright brothers' first flight. Most 747s carry a flight crew of three – Captain, Senior Flying Officer and Flight Engineer – though the latest 747 has only two crew as electronic equipment has taken over the flight engineer's job. Up to 15 cabin crew look after the passengers. On a typical flight, the takeoff weight of a 370-seater 747-200B is over 365 tonnes, of which 156 tonnes is fuel, enough to keep a car going for four years.

◁ On board BA 009 were 16 crew and 239 passengers. The lighting display was caused by friction as the plane flew through the ultra-fine ash particles.

During the long glide, radio links were weak or useless. The electronic readouts on the navigation equipment made no sense and the lights in the passenger cabins flickered on and off.

Moody turned the plane back to Java and Djakarta airport, knowing that there were mountains in the way, so if they went below 3,658 m (12,000 ft) they would have to ditch in the sea. For 12 minutes Moody flew the 747 with no power. Then, at 4,115 m (13,500 ft), an engine roared to life. Moody pulled the nose back a little and reduced the rate of descent. If he dumped some fuel he could keep flying with one engine, but there wouldn't be enough power to clear the mountains so it still meant going into the sea. Then, one by one, the other three engines started up.

Moody brought the plane safely into Djakarta, though he had to shut off an engine on the way. He could hardly see through the windshield – it had gone white and frosty, the surface etched away by the glowing sparks.

Later examination of the aircraft showed that BA 009 had flown through the ash cloud of Mt Galunggung, a volcano. The cloud had not showed up on radar because the ash particles were too small. The effect on the engines had been just like throwing sand on a fire and starting them up again was only possible after the plane had passed below the cloud.

Supersonic flight

Travelling by air became popular mostly because of its speed – an Atlantic voyage by ocean liner took up to a week. The same trip in a propeller plane took less than a day. In the 1960s, jetliners reduced the time to around seven hours and the next step was a supersonic plane, able to fly faster than sound.

The Anglo-French Concorde was the result, achieved at huge cost and after solving many technical problems. Today the Concorde is the only supersonic airliner, as the wide-body jets made cheap travel more attractive to most people than speed alone – Concorde passengers pay high fares for the luxury of high speed. The plane carries up to 128 passengers and flies at Mach 2. Mach 1, the speed of sound, is 1,062 km/h (660 mph) at Concorde's cruise height of over 18 km (11 miles).

Airline insignia

Every airline has its own colour scheme, painted on each of its aircraft. Here are the badges of some of the leading airlines. Concorde is flown by just two airlines, Air France and British Airways.

Aeroflot (USSR)   Air Canada   Air France   Alitalia (Italy)   British Airways

◁ Concorde has a drooping nose section for takeoff and landing so the flight crew can see out. In normal flight, the nose is raised level with the fuselage and a streamlined windshield covers the cockpit.

Quick and efficient turnaround

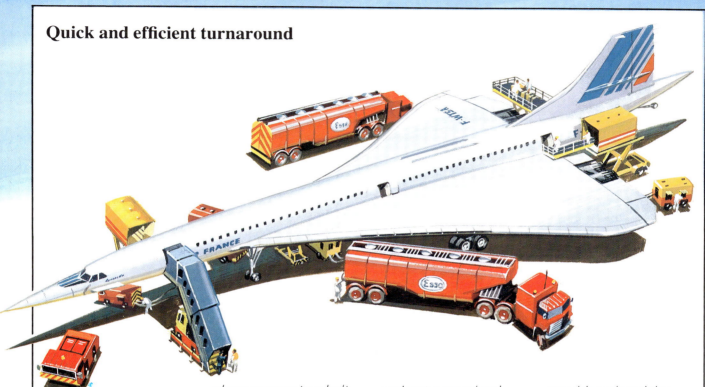

Airliners only make money while carrying passengers, so time on the ground is kept to a minimum. Concorde can be "turned around" in half an hour. As the plane comes to a halt, passengers get off in about five minutes. Tankers load 120,000 litres (26,310 gallons) of kerosene fuel in 18 minutes. Vehicles unload the baggage and put a new load aboard. Toilets are cleaned and galleys restocked with food, drink and duty-free goods. A tanker tops up the drinking water and a power truck provides electricity while the jets are shut down. When the new passengers get on board, a similar truck gives electric power for the engines to start up again.

Japan
Air
Lines

KLM
(Netherlands)

Lufthansa
(West
Germany)

Pan Am
(USA)

Qantas
(Australia)

Swissair

United
Airlines
(USA)

Air data

◁ **Benoist Type XIV**
Wingspan: 13.72 m (45 ft)
Length: 7.92 m (26 ft)
Speed: 103 km/h (64 mph)
Passengers: 1

Here are drawings of the main types of airliner described in this book. They are drawn to scale so you can compare them in size, though most airliners come in various models, so often differ slightly, as does the number of passenger seats installed.

△ **De Havilland DH 9**
Wingspan: 14 m (45 ft 11½ in)
Length: 9.22 m (30 ft 3 in)
Speed: 198 km/h (123 mph)
Passengers: 2

△ **Junkers F13**
Wingspan: 17.75 m (58 ft 3 in)
Length: 9.6 m (31 ft 6 in)
Speed: 140 km/h (87 mph)
Passengers: 4

◁ **Ford Tri-motor**
Wingspan: 22.56 m (74 ft)
Length: 15.19 m (49 ft 10 in)
Speed: 209 km/h (130 mph)
Passengers: 14

▽ **Boeing 247**
Wingspan: 22.56 m (74 ft)
Length: 15.72 m (51 ft 7 in)
Speed: 304 km/h (189 mph)
Passengers: 10

△ **Handley Page HP42E**
Wingspan: 39.62 m (130 ft)
Length: 27.36 m (89 ft 9 in)
Speed: 161 km/h (100 mph)
Passengers: 24

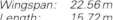

▽ **Douglas DC-3**
Wingspan: 28.9 m (95 ft)
Length: 19.63 m (64 ft 6 in)
Speed: 310 km/h (194 mph)
Passengers: 28

▽ **Short C-class Empire boat**
Wingspan: 34.77 m (114 ft)
Length: 26.84 m (88 ft)
Speed: 256 km/h (160 mph)
Passengers: 22

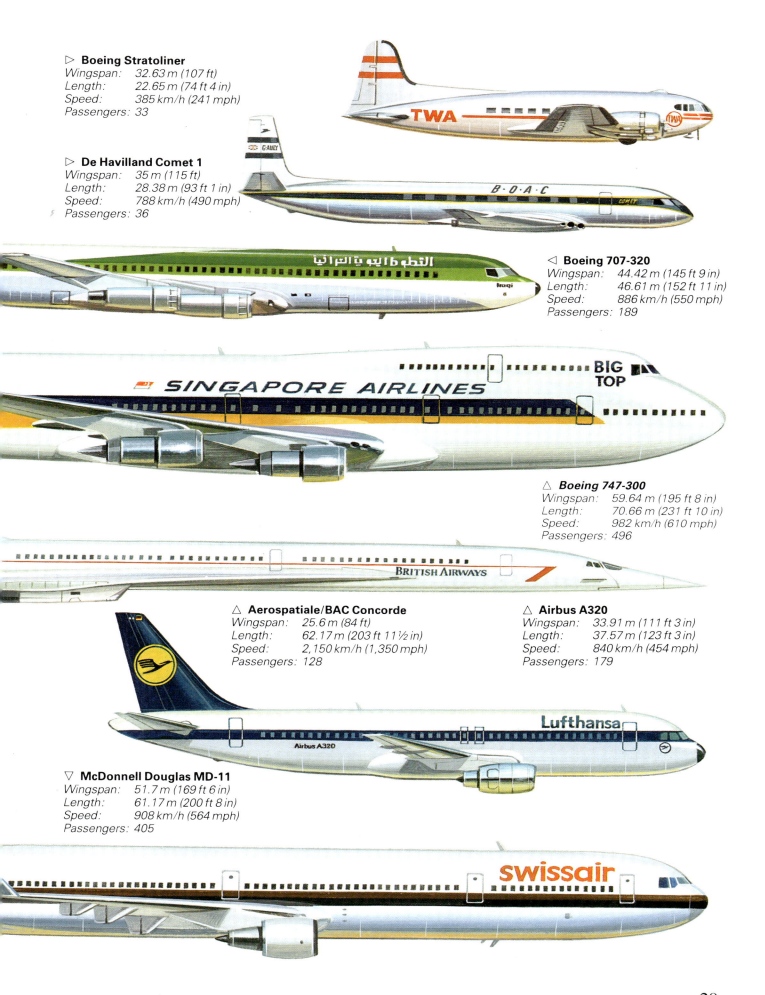

▷ **Boeing Stratoliner**
Wingspan: 32.63 m (107 ft)
Length: 22.65 m (74 ft 4 in)
Speed: 385 km/h (241 mph)
Passengers: 33

▷ **De Havilland Comet 1**
Wingspan: 35 m (115 ft)
Length: 28.38 m (93 ft 1 in)
Speed: 788 km/h (490 mph)
Passengers: 36

◁ **Boeing 707-320**
Wingspan: 44.42 m (145 ft 9 in)
Length: 46.61 m (152 ft 11 in)
Speed: 886 km/h (550 mph)
Passengers: 189

△ **Boeing 747-300**
Wingspan: 59.64 m (195 ft 8 in)
Length: 70.66 m (231 ft 10 in)
Speed: 982 km/h (610 mph)
Passengers: 496

△ **Aerospatiale/BAC Concorde**
Wingspan: 25.6 m (84 ft)
Length: 62.17 m (203 ft 11½ in)
Speed: 2,150 km/h (1,350 mph)
Passengers: 128

△ **Airbus A320**
Wingspan: 33.91 m (111 ft 3 in)
Length: 37.57 m (123 ft 3 in)
Speed: 840 km/h (454 mph)
Passengers: 179

▽ **McDonnell Douglas MD-11**
Wingspan: 51.7 m (169 ft 6 in)
Length: 61.17 m (200 ft 8 in)
Speed: 908 km/h (564 mph)
Passengers: 405

29

Inside a turbofan engine

Most modern jetliners are powered by two or more turbofan engines. The fan engine is a type of jet with a big fan at the front. A jet works like this: air is sucked in through the intake, then compressed by a series of spinning turbine blades. The compressed air is mixed with a spray of jet fuel in the combustion chamber and ignited. The hot gases roar back of the exhaust nozzle, pushing the plane forward through the air.

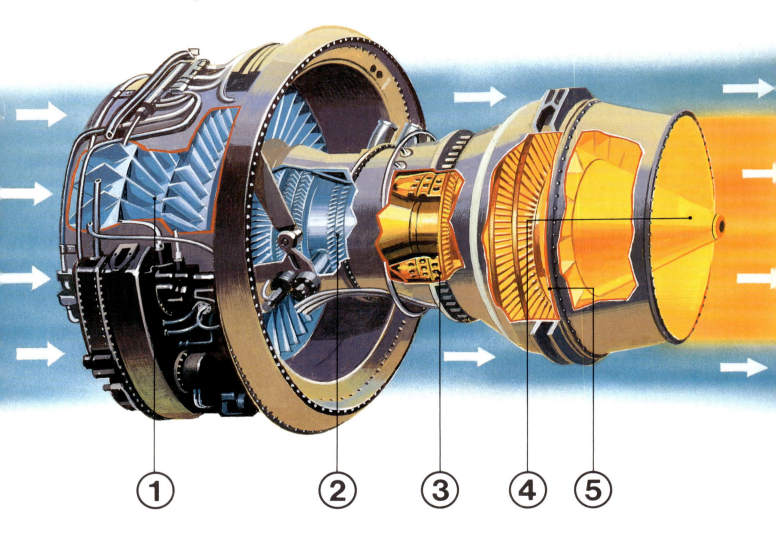

① ② ③ ④ ⑤

△ This is the Rolls-Royce RB211, a popular turbofan engine used on many aircraft, including the Boeing 747.
1 The intake fan sucks air into the compressor. Most of the air, however, is blown past the hot engine core, giving thrust just like a propeller. The cold air also surrounds the hot gas exhaust, acting as a curtain to reduce the shrieking noise which makes a pure jet (such as the Olympus used on Concorde) so painful to listen to.
2 Spinning compressor blades.
3 Air mixed with fuel and burnt in the combustion chamber.
4 Hot gases pass out of the nozzle.
5 Turbine blades spin around in the hot exhaust. The blades are connected to the front fan and compressor, keeping them spinning round.

Glossary

Biplane
An aircraft with two sets of wings, one above the other. All modern airliners are monoplanes, with just one pair of wings.

Control tower
Building in which air and ground traffic controllers work. They command all aircraft by radio and help to deal with emergencies.

De-icing fluid
Used to keep windshields ice-free. Ice forming on the wings in cloud increases the weight of a plane and reduces lift. Early aircraft had no way to combat dangerous icing, other than flying lower or avoiding icy cloud. In the 1930s, de-icing boots were invented, rubber sections wrapping round wing leading edges. Boots are blown up and down very rapidly to vibrate and crack any ice off. Modern jets use heating systems to keep wings ice-free.

Flight recorder
Machine carried in airliners to record vital statistics in flight – height, speed, crew talking and so on.

Flying boat
Aircraft with a boat-shaped fuselage, made to operate from water.

Fuselage plug
Extra section of fuselage, stretching an airliner, so increasing its passenger load. A stretched airliner usually has more powerful engines.

Galley
Naval word for kitchen, used on airliners to describe the food preparation areas. In modern jets, these are mostly reheating units for food prepared in kitchens on the ground before the flight.

Glideslope
The approach path an airliner follows on the approach to an airport. The ILS system helps a pilot keep on course.

ILS
Instrument Landing System, used to guide aircraft to a runway.

Metal fatigue
A condition which affects metal which cracks and snaps after being bent too many times. Try bending a paperclip back and forth a few times to see the effect in action.

Piston engine
Standard pre-jet engine, much like the motor used in automobiles.

Pressurized aircraft
Plane with a sealed fuselage to maintain a higher pressure than the air around. Essential at high altitude, as there is less life-giving oxygen than at ground level. At 4,267 m (14,000 ft) there is just enough oxygen if you are seated, but not enough for anything strenuous. Above this height, lack of oxygen can cause loss of consciousness and death.

Radar
Used in flight to detect other aircraft or bad weather ahead. A radar antenna in the plane's nose sends out a beam of radio waves. If the waves hit objects such as water particles in cloud, they bounce back toward the radar on the aircraft. The cloud pattern is shown on a radar screen in the cockpit.
    Airports have powerful ground radars to keep watch on the aircraft in the sky and on the runways and taxiways.

Stack
When an airport is busy, arriving aircraft are ordered to fly in circles above a radio beacon, stacked at different heights. When a runway is free, the bottom plane in the stack is guided in to land. The other planes in the stack move down a level to wait their turn for landing.

Supersonic
Faster than the speed of sound. This varies with height, from about 1,225 km/h (761 mph) at sea level to 1,062 km/h (660 mph) at high altitude.

"The pond"
Slang term for the Atlantic Ocean.

Wide-body
Airliner able to carry hundreds of passengers in rows 8–10 seats across. Cargo is mostly carried under the passenger cabins.

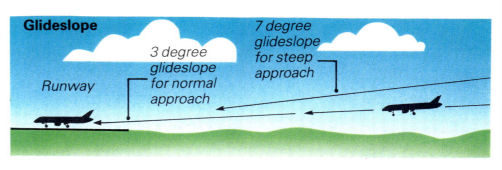

Glideslope

Runway

3 degree glideslope for normal approach

7 degree glideslope for steep approach

Index